About the Series

IDEAS IN PROGRESS is a commercially published series of working papers dealing with the alternatives to industrial society. Authors are invited to submit short monographs of work in progress of interest not only to their colleagues but also to the general public. The series fosters direct contact between the author and the reader. It provides the author with the opportunity to give wide circulation to his draft while he is still developing an idea. It offers the reader an opportunity to participate critically in shaping this idea before it has taken on a definitive form.

Future editions of the paper may include the author's revisions and critical reactions from the public. Readers are invited to write directly to the author of the present volume at the following address:

>James Robertson,
>21 Phillimore Place,
>London W8 7BY,
>England.

ABOUT THE AUTHOR

James Robertson was born in Yorkshire in 1928. He was educated in Yorkshire and Scotland, and at Oxford University. After two years in the Army and one year in the Sudan, he joined the Colonial Office as an administrative civil servant. In 1960 he accompanied Mr Harold Macmillan, then Prime Minister, on the 'wind of change' tour of Africa. From 1960 to 1963 he worked in the Cabinet Office as private secretary to the Head of the Civil Service and secretary of the Cabinet, Lord Normanbrook. He then spent two years in the Ministry of Defence.

Robertson left Whitehall in 1965 to become a consultant in computer systems analysis and management science. In 1968 he set up the Inter-Bank Research Organization (IBRO), and remained its first director until 1973. Since then he has been self-employed as a writer, lecturer, broadcaster and consultant.

In 1966 Robertson submitted an influential memorandum to the Fulton Committee on the Civil Service. In 1968/69 he was appointed to advise the Procedure Committee of the House of Commons about parliamentary control of public expenditure and taxation. In 1971 his book was published on the 'Reform of British Central Government'. In 1972 he led the IBRO team that reported on 'London's Future as an International Financial Centre'.

In the summer of 1974 Robertson's ideas on 'a non-profit society' provoked lengthy discussion, particularly in *The Sunday Times* and at a conference jointly sponsored by *The Sunday Times* and *The Science Policy Foundation.*

PROFIT OR PEOPLE?

By the same author

REFORM OF BRITISH CENTRAL GOVERNMENT

IDEAS IN PROGRESS

PROFIT OR PEOPLE?
The New Social Role of Money

James Robertson

CALDER & BOYARS

First published in Great Britain in 1974
by Calder & Boyars Limited
18 Brewer Street, London W1R 4AS

© James Robertson 1974

ALL RIGHTS RESERVED

ISBN 0 7145 0848 9 Cased Edition
ISBN 0 7145 0773 3 Paper Edition

Any paperback edition of this book whether published simultaneously with, or subsequent to, the case bound edition is sold subject to the condition that it shall not, by way of trade, be lent, resold, hired out, or otherwise disposed of, without the publishers' consent, in any form of binding other than that in which it is published.

No part of this publication may be reproduced, stored in a retrieval system, or transmitted in any form by any means, electronic, mechanical, photo-copying, recording or otherwise, except brief extracts for the purpose of review, without the prior written permission of the copyright owner and the publisher.

Printed in Great Britain
by Ebenezer Baylis and Son Limited
The Trinity Press, Worcester, and London

CONTENTS

	page
Foreword	9
Breakdown or Breakthrough	15
Socially Responsible Enterprise	23
Financially Responsible Government	40
Honest Money	62
Money Science and Money Metaphysics	77
Whose Move?	89
Bibliography	95

FOREWORD

WE cannot draw up blueprints for the society of the future. That society will be shaped by a continuing process of self-design and self-direction. It will evolve in accordance with our changing choices and values, and in conformity with the changing constraints of the world in which we live.

What the worldwide community of men and women can do—and it is now becoming urgent that we should— is to learn to use the institutions of society as effective mechanisms of collective choice, collective self-control, and collective self-determination. All institutions, including those that make up our present system of business, government and finance, have developed into their present form by an organic historical process. Our task, as I shall argue, is not to destroy this present system, or to stand on one side watching it collapse, or simply to drop out of it. Our task is to transform it. We must harness the evolutionary momentum of our institutional past to present and future needs.

The evolution of the global village, planet Earth, has become a collective learning process. Our ideas and institutions evolve as aspects of each other, and of ourselves. As our perceptions of the situation change, our institutions and procedures develop accordingly; and as the institutional mechanisms of our society change they throw up new ideas and cast fresh light on the choices before us. We are ourselves caught up in this evolutionary process. We cannot stand outside it, as Man tried to stand apart from Nature in the pre-ecological era, or as governors tried to stand apart from governed in pre-democratic days. Together with our changing ideas and institutions we must ourselves evolve collectively towards a new dimension of self-awareness and self-direction.

The ideas put forward in the following pages are intended as a contribution to that learning process. They focus on the role of money—as a social institution which could, I believe, provide one of our most important mechanisms of collective choice. They stem from my experiences—happy and unhappy—in government, industry and finance; from participation in reform of the Civil Service, Parliament, and the banks and other financial institutions of the City of London; from membership of the constantly growing fraternity of workers in business studies, computer systems analysis, and management research; and, latterly, from direct involvement in one of the many new growth points for the politics of the future. These ideas have been stimulated by discussion and argument with friends, acquaintances and colleagues in those fields. They owe much to the published ideas of others. A short bibliography is at the end.

I am very conscious that these are indeed *ideas in progress*. I hope there may be social scientists, lawyers, ecologists, information scientists, urban planners, political philosophers, accountants, control engineers, ethologists, games theorists, economists and other professional thinkers, in whose minds they will strike a spark. Although I am not at home in any of their fields, I know that the ideas sketched here could fruitfully associate with theirs. I hope that what I say may ring true also to many ordinary people who, being outsiders to the—still, alas—closed worlds of big business, high finance and central government, may sometimes wonder why the system of money values is so much out of line with the system of values which people actually hold. Finally, in a more explicitly political sense, I hope that these ideas will appeal to people who care about causes and interests that are bound to go largely unrepresented so long as our society is governed by alternating parties of big business and organized labour, both of which are obsessed with profit. Many such people —for example, consumerists and conservationists—are already laying the foundations for the breakthrough to the post-capitalist, post-socialist society of the future—a society where profit will have a very different role, if any, from the role it has played hitherto.

When Marion Boyars invited me to contribute to *Ideas In Progress*, I was excited by the thought that readers would be encouraged to participate in the further development of the ideas put forward. With that in view I hope it will be helpful at the outset to pinpoint some of the main questions that arise.

First, clearer definitions are needed of the terms 'socially responsible enterprise', 'financially responsible government' and an 'honest money system'. Such definitions must be operational. In other words they will consist in the introduction of new practices and procedures in business, government and the financial sector. What I intend to convey by these terms is that the time has come to clarify the functions and responsibilities of commercial enterprises, government departments and financial institutions; that these organizations should now assume explicit responsibility for serving the interests of all the parties directly involved in their activities, and for contributing to the well-being of the kind of society that is widely accepted as fair; and that they should carry out their functions openly and honestly—taking continual care to show that they are indeed meeting all their responsibilities. The changes I shall suggest in the legal structure of companies, in governmental procedures for handling public cash flows under parliamentary supervision, and in the operations of the financial sector, should therefore be taken as an initial attempt to define 'socially responsible enterprise', 'financially responsible government', and 'an honest money system'. More detailed definition will have to be provided by industrialists and business managers, civil servants and parliamentarians, and bankers and financial people, working out and putting into practice the measures needed if we are to move in this direction. While we are on definitions, I should make it clear that the term 'money system' is intended to include all the monetary and financial institutions in both the private and the public sector which provide the monetary infrastructure and the financial services needed by modern society and its members. One of the main suggestions made is that those institutions should now be required to work in ways that are demonstrably honest and fair. Perhaps I should also make it clear that by 'free enterprise', for example in the term 'socially responsible free enterprise', I intend to convey the idea that we shall be able to restore greater autonomy to individual enterprises and re-validate the authority of business managements, once we have clarified their social responsibilities. I do not mean by 'free enterprise' a business system whose primary aim is to make profits for shareholders.

Second, it may be difficult to grasp immediately the idea that, for practical purposes, we ought to discard the economic concepts of profit and surplus. Most people have been conditioned to thinking that a business has to meet certain inescapable financial expenditures out of the available funds and that what remains thereafter is residual profit or surplus. They are not accustomed to thinking in terms of allocating *all* the available funds to various purposes according to collective decisions made on behalf of *all* the various interests concerned. They feel the need for a proof that there is no such thing as profit or surplus, before they will willingly discard the concepts. So it may be helpful to stress the pragmatic nature of what I am suggesting. That is that it is now desirable to adopt new conventions and new procedures for dealing with the money flowing through a business, and for allocating it so as to meet all the obligations of the business in ways that are accepted as fair. Again, questions of definition arise. And again the detailed definition of a non-profit economy will be operational. It will involve the development of new procedures for business planning and financial management by practical business people who accept the need to change the existing conventions.

Third, I recognize that a deep gulf lies between those who basically believe in openness and freedom, and those who basically do not. There are some people who believe it should be possible to create a society in which free people would be glad to co-operate with one another and treat one another fairly. There are others who believe that most people will cheat and exploit their fellows if they are given the freedom to do so. The latter foresee a Chilean disintegration to political extremes and an eventual suspension of democracy, as the economic, social and political problems of modern societies grow more serious and the divisions and antagonisms within them grow more violent. The former recognize the risk of disaster, but they conclude—as a matter of realism, not idealism—that the only feasible way to tackle these problems, including inflation, is to create a greater sense of openness and fairness and involvement among society's members. It is important to recognize this basic difference of temperament and attitude, and to accept that it exists. But, having done so, it is necessary to consider whether the functions of business, government and finance will not have to be clarified and re-defined in some such way as I am suggesting, whichever point of view one takes. Even people who intuitively feel that imposed solutions will be inevitable in the end, may have valuable contributions to make to the process of clarification and re-definition.

Fourthly and lastly, the question arises whether what I am trying to say is applicable in one country only. I have been asked, 'Is this a prescription for Britain, for Europe, or for the World?' Clearly the links between different countries are now so close in industrial, commercial, financial and governmental matters that the scope for one country like Britain to go it alone is limited. Moreover the problems faced by Britain are shared with many other countries. If these ideas are relevant in Britain, they must be relevant in other countries too. So, although the institutions discussed are specifically British, I shall be disappointed if the discussion is not more widely relevant, and I look forward with special interest to comments and reactions from other countries. At the same time, however, I must confess to a mildly chauvinistic hope that this is a sphere in which Britain may prove to have a pioneering role.

BREAKDOWN OR BREAKTHROUGH

THE fabric of advanced society appears to be breaking down. For us that is the overriding problem of our times. But it is a problem for the whole world. The money system is central to it.

Private capitalism and state socialism are obsolete. The kind of politics that is based on conflict between the two is becoming increasingly discredited. So is the kind of economy that is based on compromise between the two. The peoples of the world—rich and poor, developed and developing—are trying to go beyond the struggle between capital and labour. They are searching for a fruitful union between the best of free enterprise and the best of socialism. They have had enough of destructive conflict or sterile compromise between the worst of both.

In Britain the old mould is certainly breaking. This is what elitists mean when they say Britain is becoming ungovernable. But, as the twilight of the old ideologies grows deeper and the existing system is tested to destruction, it is not the elitists who matter.

'You're all the same, the lot of you—feathering

your own nests.' That message came through loud and clear to all who knocked on people's doors during the British general election of February 1974. They were not talking primarily about corruption. They felt crushed between the big trade unions, big business, big government, and the big banks, building societies and financial institutions of the City of London. Industrial stoppages, short-time working, the pay freeze in its various stages, rising rents and rates and prices, high interest rates, the mortgage crisis, record bank profits, the recent property bonanza—all these were seen as the outcome of a struggle between remote and powerful institutions which had run out of control. And in this situation public men and women generally were seen to be playing the system and looking after themselves.

Britain is going through a deep-seated crisis of credibility in business, finance, government and politics. In my view, this lack of credibility is well justified. For example, company law is badly out of date; remote shareholders cause 'absentee landlord' problems for large corporations; small private companies—which should be growing points of enterprise and innovation—are discouraged. The financial system favours those who run it against those who use it; big people against small; borrowers against savers; and those who speculate in existing assets against those who invest productively. The tax and social security systems perversely combine economic inefficiency with social unfairness; in the richer, the middling and the poorer reaches of society alike they penalize thrift and hard work; at the same time, tax concessions and social security benefits often seem to favour those who do not need help more than those who do. The administrative and parliamentary routines for planning and managing public expenditure, taxation and government borrowing—and using them openly as instruments for settling social and economic priorities in accordance with public opinion expressed through Parliament—are years behind the times.

At a deeper level, changes are taking place all the world over that point in an entirely different direction from the big business and big government orthodoxies of modern capitalism and modern socialism. These changes point towards a form of society in which there will have to be greater scope for personal freedom and personal initiative than there is today, within a stronger framework of social justice; a society that will have to be pluralistic but systematically ordered, decentralized but socially responsible; a society that will have to be able to plan ahead better than is possible today, while becoming more open and self-governing; a society in which the emphasis will continue to shift away from economic and commercial objectives towards social and environmental goals, away from the continually growing consumption of natural resources towards their conservation, away from the constantly increasing production of *things* towards the provision of better services and amenities for *people*; a society which will regard personal values more highly than institutional loyalties, and will require its institutions to serve its people rather than its people to serve its institutions.

This secular shift of values has been signalled by

Ivan Illich in *Celebration of Awareness*, *Deschooling Society*, and elsewhere; by Charles Reich in *The Greening of America*; by the 'limits to growth' school of ecologists and conservationists; and by many others in recent years.

Almost all these thinkers have noted the tendency of established institutions—education services, health services, social services, transport systems, large business corporations, banks, government departments, public agencies, and political parties—to turn into self-serving and self-perpetuating bureaucracies. Personal experience, too, confirms that top people in government, business and finance in Britain today have become prisoners of the systems which they are supposed to shape in the service of society's changing needs. They are not necessarily to blame for that, but it is a fact. I doubt if many of them would deny that the last few years have been rather inglorious.

Established institutions acquire a life and momentum of their own. Today our institutions are rather like a huge ocean liner, seemingly out of control, locked on course, and moving steadily in the wrong direction. The ship's officers spend most of their time arguing about one another's mistakes. The crew and the more alert among the passengers are becoming alarmed, and their protesting voices can be heard. Some advise jumping overboard. Some think only to destroy the ship. The rest of us are confused, not only by these counsels of despair, but also by a number of false options that we seem to be offered. A prosperous society *or* a fair one? Economic growth *or* social justice? Personal freedom *or* social responsibility? Good government *or* democracy?

These are bogus dilemmas. But they will only disappear if we can transform our systems of government and money into genuine mechanisms of collective choice. We have to develop socially responsible self-government right through society— at every level and in every walk of life. By that approach, and—I believe—by that approach only, we can master the controls and turn the big ship round.

Elsewhere, in the context of government reform, I have suggested that we have already entered the early, confused stages of a fundamental revolution in business and finance, government and politics. This revolution is like a scientific revolution.

Revolutions happen in science when an old theory outlives its usefulness. As a long-standing scientific theory becomes more and more complicated, it becomes less and less effective as an instrument of scientific discovery and explanation. In the 15th and 16th centuries the Ptolemaic system of astronomy could be reconciled with newly observed facts only by making more and more detailed qualifications and reservations to it. Eventually it was bound to crumble beneath their weight. A new vision of the universe was needed—a new perspective which the new facts would fit. The Copernican revolution had to come. When it did come it was very simple: the sun does not go round the world; the world goes round the sun. Similarly, there comes a time when piecemeal changes in the institutions of society reach the limit of their usefulness, and patching things up only makes matters worse. When that happens, a new conception is needed of the purpose of politics and government, business and finance, and all society's institutions; a new theory, almost, against which society's current problems will fall clearly into place; a new key, which makes it possible to tackle those problems in a coherent way.

That time is upon us now. I believe that, in the constitutional and the economic sphere alike, the key concept for the future is socially responsible self-government.

In the constitutional sphere, Scottish, Welsh and now Ulster nationalism, English regionalism and local community politics, have been emerging as major features of the British political scene in the last few years. Thus in Britain as in other countries people have been reacting against closed, remote, centralized government and demanding a bigger say in running their own affairs. Meanwhile, many detailed reforms of government organization have been introduced or proposed. There have been the Fulton reforms of the civil service, constant changes in the machinery of central government, various reforms of Parliament, wholesale reorganization of local government after the Redcliffe-Maud Report, and now more recently there has been the Kilbrandon Report on constitutional changes. But all these changes have been conceived piecemeal and, for the most part, paternalistically. Only when we come to see them in perspective, as steps towards more systematic and more open methods of self-government at every level, will they fall into place as related parts of a coherent programme of institutional reform—together with many other proposals for improving present procedures and practice, such as: televising the proceedings of Parliament; setting up a parliamentary select committee in the sphere of financial administration; developing open, systematic routines to enable the public to participate in local planning; and introducing electoral reforms.

However, our present concern is not so much with these constitutional questions as with the economic sphere—business, industry, finance, industrial relations, industrial investment, prices, incomes, and so forth. Here the most obvious counterpart to Celtic nationalism and community politics has been the growth of militant trade unionism over the last few years—the shift of power to the shop floor. Successive Labour and Conservative governments have tried to impose legal restrictions on the trade union movement and centralized controls over incomes; both have been heavily defeated. As in the constitutional field, numerous piecemeal changes across the whole range of business and the economy —prices and incomes boards and commissions, tax changes, reforms in banking and finance, consumer protection, investment incentives for industry, monopolies and mergers policies, and many other measures introduced in recent years—seem to have made confusion worse confounded. Again, it now seems clear that all our multifarious and intractable problems in the economic sphere will only fall into perspective—and solutions to them will only begin to emerge—once we accept the need to develop business and finance into mechanisms of socially responsible self-government.

John Rawls has recently said that 'the theory of justice is part of the theory of rational choice'. My theme here is that the money system is one of society's chief mechanisms of collective choice. The breakthrough we are looking for will depend on our reshaping the money system, along with our other institutions, into fit mechanisms of choice for a post-capitalist and post-socialist society which is accepted by its members as just and fair.

SOCIALLY RESPONSIBLE ENTERPRISE

'THERE is no pain like the pain of a new idea'—except, William James might have added, the pain of scrapping an old one. Nonetheless, the idea that the primary function of large business corporations is to maximize—or even to optimize—profits for shareholders is obsolete. In practice big business managements no longer subscribe to it. But its myth still creates deeply felt antagonisms. It is a heavy millstone round industry's neck.

In spite of some recent short-term fluctuations, the profits returned by British industry have been falling steadily over the last quarter of a century. Inflation and the size of government financial aid to industry make the situation even worse than appears at first sight. It is possible to argue about the precise figures, but undoubtedly the long-term trend for industrial profits is poor. At the same time, profit has become a dirty word for more and more people, and there is no sign that the business community will be able to rehabilitate it. Again, it is a matter of fact—a matter of power politics—that the trade unions can now bring the country to a halt whenever it seems reasonable to their members and their members' families for them to do so. All this will make it impossible to restore a healthy, viable economy, if we cling to the notion that big business exists to make profits for shareholders.

This judgement is confirmed by the whole series of changes—loosely interrelated as yet—which are forcing companies to become more 'socially responsible'. Everyone accepts that company law reform is overdue, and most people now accept that reform will have to be a good deal more far-reaching than Mr Heath and Mr Walker intended, as Prime Minister and Secretary of State for Trade and Industry in the Conservative government of 1970 to 1974. Recent 'fair trading' legislation has significantly increased the potential strength of consumer protection law. Employee protection has been strengthened by 'contracts of employment' legislation, and may be further strengthened by whatever emerges now that the Industrial Relations Act has been repealed. At the same time, legal controls over pollution and other forms of industrial damage to the environment are growing stronger. In all these ways new pieces of the jigsaw are falling into place and a comprehensive statutory framework is beginning to emerge for the control of business activities. The work being done on 'social responsibilities' and codes of conduct by the Confederation of British Industry (CBI), the British Institute of Management (BIM), and similar bodies is another sign of the times.

This is the context in which such issues as two-tier boards, worker directors and industrial democracy have taken on immediate importance. As further changes take place along these lines, the responsibilities of company boards to parties other than the shareholders will loom larger. The special status of shareholders, relatively to other stakeholders in the company, is bound to be downgraded. The idea that the company exists to create maximum profits for shareholders is bound to lose conviction. The myth that large companies like ICI are 'owned' by their shareholders will be explicitly discarded.

What are we to put in its place? For practical purposes in Britain today there appear to be three possibilities: state socialism, with the trade union leaders in a dominant role; corporate statism, with the financial institutions dominant; or socially responsible free enterprise.

I shall be arguing that the third is to be preferred. But, to avoid misunderstanding as the discussion proceeds, three points should be stressed. On none of them is there any reason for the realist and the idealist to disagree.

First, there is no doubt that many people are motivated by the hope of making money, of securing material reward, and of attaining the status that goes with money and material wealth. It may be true that, as society becomes more prosperous and better educated, increasing numbers of able people will be motivated by non-material incentives. But, if people feel underpaid compared with their fellows, they feel unfairly treated. Money will always be, in Herzberg's phrase, an important 'hygiene factor'. For this reason, if for no other, in reshaping the institutions of our society we must give fuller scope to more people's material aspirations. This is, indeed, one of the most important respects in which the present situation has to be improved.

Second, as Schumacher has it, small is beautiful. The scope for small enterprises, including small commercial companies, must be widened—not reduced. They suffer disadvantage and discouragement in an economy dominated by big business, big government and big trade unions, and enmeshed in institutionalized complexity. They should be vital growing points for a flourishing economy and for continuing innovation. They can perform a valuable social function too, by enabling people to lead more independent lives than is possible for those who are tied to the career ladders of large organizations, however high they may climb.

Third, the concepts of 'fairness' and 'justice' must be handled with care. It is not possible to lay down absolutely or objectively what is fair. Fairness will always be subjective to some extent; and to some extent, ours will always be an unfair world. It should therefore be clearly understood that in the present context to talk about fairness or justice is to talk about institutional procedures and not about metaphysics. When I say that fairness should replace profit maximization as the primary aim of business and that fairness should take over from maximum economic growth as the primary aim of government, I mean that for practical purposes the first priority in business and in government should henceforth be to secure genuine acceptance and consent from *all* the parties whose interests may be affected by what business and government do.

We can examine these questions more systematically, with the aid of the simplified diagram overleaf. The enterprise is shown as a 'system'. The arrows represent flows of money. The enterprise could equally be a shareholder company, a consumer co-operative, an employee co-operative, or a nationalized industry. All have responsibilities to investors, customers, employees and the government, though the primary legal responsibility varies in each case.*

One social mechanism determines the character of the enterprise; another governs its activities in a different way. The first is the Law. The second is Money. The Law lays down the framework of rules defining the rights and obligations of the enterprise towards the various interested parties, their rights and obligations towards it, and their relative status. Money constrains the activities of the enterprise in a more straightforward way: the money flowing into it must balance the money flowing out.

The function of the money system is, in brief, to provide a calculus—a scoring system—to indicate the entitlement of members of society to purchasing power, and thus the claims they may make on society's resources. If this scoring system is working efficiently and fairly, each enterprise will receive a

* I shall treat these four (i.e. excluding suppliers in most normal cases) as the main parties with an interest in the enterprise. Other interested parties, such as creditors or the local communities directly affected by an enterprise's activities are not shown. They are important but, to simplify the argument, creditors may be regarded as a special category of 'suppliers' (or of 'investors'), while local communities' interests may be regarded as one of the responsibilities of 'government'.

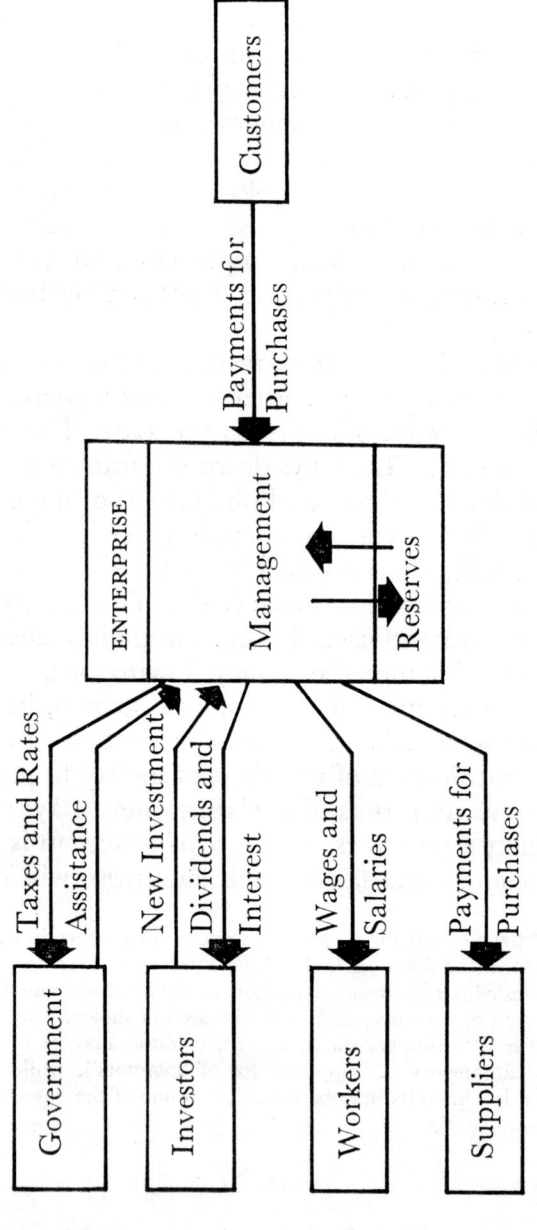

Figure 1

flow of money commensurate with the contribution it makes to society's well-being by producing goods and services that people value. Then, if the internal arrangements of the enterprise are working efficiently and fairly for distributing the outgoing flows of money among the various parties involved —including employees and investors—they too will receive flows of money commensurate with their contribution to the enterprise as a whole.

The basic model of the enterprise is thus very simple. No mention of 'profit'; no mention of 'ownership'; merely laws to lay down the rules of the game, money to provide the scoring system, and management to see that the enterprise survives and carries out its responsibilities to all the parties involved.

Our present troubles can now be explained as follows. In recent years the struggle between capital and labour has resulted in control seeping away from the individual enterprise to the trade unions, the financial institutions and central government. The adversary system of industrial relations between trade unions representing employees and management representing shareholders (who now tend to be financial institutions instead of individual investors) has gone far to destroy the authority of managements and boards of directors. This tug-of-war has also put pressure on prices, since the obvious way to give more money to employees without taking it from shareholders has been to take it from customers. Successive governments, for their part, have failed to exercise the degree of monetary control that would have kept prices down; they too have been trying to get a quart out of a pint pot; they have borrowed heavily, thereby injecting into the economy the new money that has made price rises possible. This has meant that, in order to control inflation, governments have been forced to intervene directly by imposing detailed centralized controls over prices and incomes.

We now find, therefore, that the flows of money entering and leaving the individual enterprise, as shown in Figure 1—prices from customers, prices to suppliers, salaries and wages to employees, and dividends to investors—are largely determined by remote control. This is bound to be unhealthy. Trade unions, financial institutions, and departments of central government feel little direct responsibility for the individual enterprises which they bear down upon so heavily. It is no wonder in the circumstances if company boards and managements feel a diminished sense of commercial initiative and social responsibility.

The present structure of political debate compounds these problems. The division between Conservative and Labour—capitalism and socialism—is almost literally pulling our present industrial economy apart. Between 1970 and 1974 Mr Heath's Conservative government committed itself to a form of highly centralized corporate state. It brought pressure upon the big financial institutions to exercise greater influence on industry and it developed highly centralized arrangements for the detailed control of prices, salaries and wages, and dividends.

It left office after being defeated in a confrontation with the miners and the trade unions. The Labour government that replaced it in March 1974 was committed to a form of centralized state socialism in which the trade unions—rather than the financial institutions—were to be the main focus of industrial power, and in which the National Enterprise Board and 'planning agreements' between the government and big companies would exert central control over the industrial economy.

I am arguing that a third course is preferable. Instead of the big business, big finance, big trade union, big government orthodoxies of the Conservative and Labour parties, we should aim to develop decentralized, socially responsible, autonomous enterprises which no longer purport to be in business primarily to maximize profit for shareholders. This means re-defining the boundary between the public and private sectors, not by nationalization but by developing large public companies into socially responsible, self-governing enterprises. We should revive the worker-oriented philosophy of Owenite socialism, the customer-oriented philosophy of the co-operative movement, and the traditional business philosophy of the small entrepreneur; and we should weave these strands into the fabric of a post-capitalist, post-socialist, free enterprise economy which is directly responsible to society.

So, how can we return control to individual enterprises, and revalidate the authority of business managements?

The first need is to build into the internal control

structure of the enterprise the necessary mechanisms to ensure that it discharges—and is seen to discharge —*all* its social responsibilities. It follows that the supreme authority must rest with a governing body —a board—that recognizes multiple responsibilities. From that it follows that there should be two boards —a supervisory board and a management board. The supervisory board will provide the valid authority that managements must have by balancing the interests of the various parties involved in the enterprise, by resolving conflicts between them, by ensuring that all the company's responsibilities are met, and by setting management objectives accordingly.

In reforming company law to meet these needs, many detailed questions of what Gladstone called 'a dry and repulsive kind' will have to be considered. How are we to safeguard the interests of all the parties concerned? How are representatives of the various interests to be selected to serve on the supervisory board? By appointment or election? In what numbers? How are they to be accountable? How are decisions to be reached by the supervisory board? By simple majority voting, or according to more complicated procedures? How are relations between the supervisory and the management boards to be defined? These questions are already under discussion in many countries, including Britain. In some, like Germany and Holland, experience of two-tier boards is already mounting up. However, I suggest that the essential point is for the directing body of every enterprise, whether company, nationalized industry, school or hospital, to contain non-executive members personally charged with representing the interests of the employees, the customers, the investors, and the public. In total those members should have a voting majority on the board; that is to say, they should be able to outvote the executive directors and other directors representing the management's point of view. Although they might not necessarily be elected, they should be held publicly accountable. Their leadership should be seen as a form of stewardship. They will thus be expected to apply methods of *efficiency audit*, *social audit* and *financial audit*, which will enable them to demonstrate openly and clearly that the enterprise is meeting its obligations towards employees, customers, investors and the public. Auditors will, logically, be appointed by the director (or directors) responsible for representing the public interest on the supervisory board.

Many detailed financial questions also arise, once we accept that the objective of large companies is not, after all, to maximize profits for shareholders. These concern the volume and the apportionment of the funds flowing through the enterprise. Which of the parties are to be exposed to financial uncertainty and risk? As financial inflows and outflows fluctuate, which outflows are to be fixed and which variable? According to what formulae are they to vary? What financial claims shall each of the parties be able to make, if the business has to be wound up? What methods of planning and monitoring, controlling and accounting for these flows of funds shall be adopted? Who shall control the prices charged, and the incomes generated, by the business? How are we to reward people who shoulder the risks, uncertainties and fluctuations that affect all businesses? How are we to attract new investment in industry? How are we to safeguard the legitimate interests of shareholders, as more and more ordinary people entrust their savings, their insurance and their pensions to shareholding institutions? How are we to build in decentralized counter-inflationary controls at the level of the socially responsible enterprise?

The key concept here is the concept of cash flows and cash flow management. Essentially this is very simple. It is based on the obvious fact that the streams of money flowing into an enterprise—or an individual's bank account, or the government Exchequer—have to balance the streams of money flowing out.

At a technical level it is already becoming accepted that control of the flows of money entering and leaving a business (as shown in Figure 1) is more important for the survival and healthy development of the business than the calculation of profits and losses in the traditional way. 'Annual income twenty pounds, annual expenditure nineteen nineteen six, result happiness. Annual income twenty pounds, annual expenditure twenty pounds ought and six, result misery.' Mr Micawber knew that cash flow was all-important; no fancy calculations of profitability for him. Similarly, modern business managements now recognize that cash flow planning, cash flow management, and cash flow accounting are the vital elements on the financial side. Profit calculations can very easily obscure the true position and prospects of a business, whereas cash flow projections will reveal them.

As the multiple obligations of company managements to workers, investors, customers and the general public become more clearly established, financial planning will be increasingly concerned with balancing cash flows coming in and cash flows going out, and with distributing outgoing cash flows in a manner acceptable to all the stakeholders. Company managements will thus think of themselves as 'buying' whatever finance they need from investors and lenders at going market rates. So far as fixed interest borrowing is concerned, no new problem will arise. But the basis for risk finance will change. The return will still have to be variable. But it will have to be specified according to a formula agreed between the company and the investor, possibly as a rate of return proportionate to total turnover; this rate of return will have to be acceptable to the other stakeholders in the enterprise; the investor will not be an 'owner' of the company, and there will be no suggestion that the company is in business primarily to maximize the return on his investment. Nonetheless, the investor can still be given a secure claim to a return that varies according to the company's success, and there is no reason why this claim should not be traded on the Stock Exchange just like securities of traditional kinds. These arrangements will require the analysis of risks and commensurate rewards to be a good deal more sophisticated than it generally is today. The basis on which existing shareholdings can fairly be converted to new forms of risk-bearing or fixed-interest securities will be a complicated matter to decide. Changes in Stock Exchange procedures and other related procedures for dealing in the new kinds of bonds and securities will also be necessary. But these are points of technical detail, largely for the financial experts to work out.

Next, where are investment funds to come from? As Figure 1 shows, there are three possible sources: funds retained by the company in its own reserves; new funds supplied by investors, including new money borrowed by the company from banks and other sources of loans; and financial assistance from the government. There is no reason why any particular enterprise should not be flexible about raising investment money from all three sources. But each has the following important implications for the overall pattern of cash flows through society, and therefore for the distribution of spending power among society's members, and thus of the right to participate in collective decisions and collective choices about the use of resources.

If companies are generally expected to rely on retained finance, this means that managements are expected to retain for themselves significant powers to determine the future allocation of the resources available to society and to influence the distribution of spending power among society's members. They lose those powers if the cash flowing through their businesses is generously distributed to employees by way of increased salaries and wages, to investors by way of a higher return on their investment, and (in a negative sense) to customers by reductions in prices. Those who favour retained finance as a main source of investment funds are, therefore, of the opinion that corporate choices and decisions made by business managers are likely to serve the public interest better than individual choices widely dispersed. That view is held by many top businessmen and, paradoxically, by many socialists.

If, on the other hand, companies are expected to rely on government sources of investment finance, this means that funds must be channelled to industry from the general public through the government in the form of taxes or government borrowing. The implication here is that choices made by politicians and civil servants at central government level about the allocation of resources and the distribution of purchasing power are likely to be preferable—from the point of view of the general interest—to choices made in a more pluralistic way by individual and corporate members of society at large. That view is held by many top civil servants and politicians, as well as by many socialists. The danger, of course, is that civil servants and politicians tend to think of the tax-paying public as a bottomless well of money, and to exert much less effective disciplines over public spending and the selection of spending priorities than if the money was their own. This danger affects the traditional public services as well as the nationalized industries.

Finally, if companies are expected to rely principally on raising new funds from investors and lenders—having themselves previously distributed the cash flows generated by their businesses to their employees, investors and customers—the implication is that the general interest will be served best if the power of choice about the allocation of resources and spending power is widely spread—and continually re-spread—among individual people. That is the democratic view.

The latter course has much to commend it. It is the least paternalistic approach so far as company managements and the government are concerned. It involves maximum involvement by individuals in society's affairs, both as stakeholders in their enterprise and as potential savers and investors. But it does require the financial institutions to operate efficiently and fairly as mechanisms for collecting the savings of people and investing them to create new social and economic welfare and well-being.

My thesis, then, is that socially responsible free enterprise is preferable to centralized state socialism or the corporate state. I am sure that by adopting it as our goal we could do much to defuse the antagonisms that now pull industry apart. I have sketched what it might mean at the level of the individual enterprise. But it cannot be achieved without corresponding changes in government and in the money system as a whole. These, including the problem of inflation, are discussed in the chapters that follow. Two points remain to be stressed.

First, it will not be enough to redefine the responsibilities of companies only, and to clarify the accountability only of company boards. The same need applies to the financial system, the trade union movement, and the government bureaucracies. In each of these three cases we now find largely self-regulating, closed institutions—all of which, to a very considerable extent, are a law unto themselves, and all of which tend to resist being made more openly accountable to Parliament and to the public under the law. They too must have their social responsibilities clarified and be brought within a framework of social control, if individual enterprises are to preserve their autonomy from undue outside intervention. Effective measures are necessary to regulate the financial institutions of the City and the big trade unions, and to strengthen parliamentary supervision over the civil service.

Second, I have already suggested the need for a radical re-appraisal of the mixed economy as we know it today, and a big change in our ideas about the dividing line between the public and the private sector. This point will be discussed further under the heading 'Money Science and Money Metaphysics'.

Writing of the pre-capitalist, pre-socialist age R. H. Tawney said, 'To found a science of society upon the assumption that the appetite for economic gain is a constant and measurable force, to be accepted like other natural forces as an inevitable and self-evident datum, would have appeared to the medieval thinker as hardly less irrational or less immoral than to make the premise of social philosophy the unrestrained operation of such necessary human attributes as pugnacity or the sexual instinct.' That seems a fitting thought with which to end this outline of the socially responsible, self-governing enterprise of the post-capitalist, post-socialist society that is now beginning to emerge.

FINANCIALLY RESPONSIBLE GOVERNMENT

So much, then, for the social responsibilities of enterprises. The time is coming when undertakings of all kinds, including industrial firms and financial concerns, will no longer be organized and controlled on the assumption that they exist to maximize something called 'profits' for shareholders. They will be expected to plan and manage their activities in such a way that all the interested parties can co-operate, with sufficient assurance that the resulting benefits will be fairly shared. Moreover, the country's money system should be regarded as society's mechanism for allocating resources and distributing purchasing power among its members. This means that, like individual enterprises, the financial system will be expected to operate openly and accountably—to enable all concerned to see for themselves that it is working fairly and efficiently. I shall have more to say about that in the next chapter.

We now turn, however, to the financial responsibilities of the government. Our hypothesis is that, once industrial and financial concerns are openly operating as socially responsible free enterprises—

and meeting society's needs within a clearly understood framework of law and public policy, coherently designed and openly administered by government authorities—it will become unnecessary as well as undesirable for the government to intervene in their affairs in detail. Further, we postulate that government's primary aim is not to maximize at the national level something called 'economic growth', corresponding to 'profit' in the business context, but to provide a framework within which economic and social benefits can be co-operatively created and fairly distributed. So, like business concerns and financial institutions, government too will increasingly be expected to plan and manage its activities openly and accountably—in this case under the supervision of Parliament—in such a way that all concerned can see for themselves how economic and social benefits can be created co-operatively and whether they are indeed being fairly shared.

In other words, we postulate a three-tier model of business, government and Parliament. Socially responsible *industrial firms and financial concerns* with a large measure of self-management will be expected to do their business competitively and openly, in a market shaped by a framework of law and public policy openly administered by *government departments and agencies*, under the supervision of *Parliament*—which will itself be expected to work openly, for example by broadcasting its proceedings and giving the public access to them in other ways.

Against that background we need to define the responsibilities of government for using, maintaining and developing the money system as an effective mechanism of collective choice and self-determination.

There are four separate, though related tasks for the government in the monetary and financial sphere.

> First, it must plan and manage its own cash flows. Public expenditure, taxation and government borrowing are the cash flows under its direct control.
>
> Second, the government is responsible for the efficient and proper working of the monetary and financial system in society at large. It must carry out the functions of central monetary authority and take responsibility for regulating the financial markets.
>
> Third, the government must legislate as necessary to protect the interests of those who deal with financial institutions, just as it has a duty to safeguard the legitimate interests of all customers, employees and investors.
>
> Fourth, insofar as the financial services industry is an important industry from the national viewpoint, the government should pay regard to the commercial interests of financial institutions.

We need to concern ourselves only with the first three tasks; if they are properly carried out the fourth will fall into place.

Cash Flows

The diagram overleaf gives a simplified picture of the government's cash flows.

How are we to arrange for these flows of expenditure, taxation and borrowing to be planned and managed openly and clearly, in a manner acceptable to all concerned? What procedures shall we adopt for ensuring that the government plans and manages them as instruments for settling and carrying out agreed social and economic priorities at the national level—in other words, as effective mechanisms of collective choice?

First, the channels through which money flows should be clearly understandable to all; the amounts flowing through them should be openly apparent; and the resulting pattern of cash flows through society should be visible to all as the reflection of the pattern of social and economic activity that society has chosen to develop. This means, for example, that when the government wishes to provide financial assistance to people or organizations on grounds of public policy, for example by subsidizing loans for house purchase, it should do so openly by public expenditure under parliamentary supervision. It should not do so by distorting the financial markets (for example, by giving special tax advantages to concerns like 'building societies'). It should not do so by giving tax concessions that result in richer people getting more assistance than poorer people. It should not do so by borrowing money for itself more cheaply than at the true market rates, whether through the Bank of England or the National

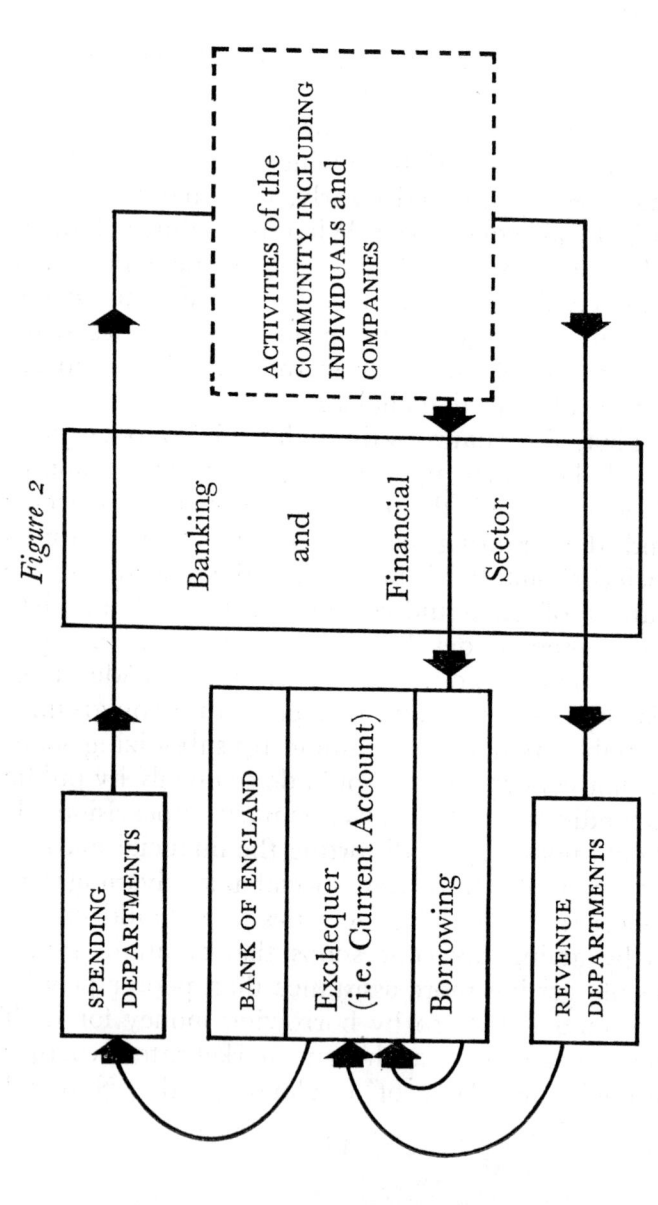

Figure 2

Savings Bank. Subsidies to lenders to encourage saving, or to borrowers to encourage particular forms of spending, should be made clearly out of the public purse—if, indeed, they are necessary at all.

As well as ensuring that the mechanisms of government spending, revenue raising, and borrowing are clear and easily understood, it is also necessary to arrange for these government cash flows to be planned and managed and accounted for in a manner which Parliament and the public can easily understand. Briefly, the Treasury should be made openly responsible and called to account for preparing and publishing forward projections of public expenditure, taxation, and borrowing five years ahead, as background to its annual budgetary proposals for expenditure, taxation and borrowing during the coming year. As part of Parliament's regular annual routine these projections should be examined as a whole by a new select committee on financial administration, and then be debated by the House of Commons. An arrangement on these lines will give Parliament and the public an opportunity to consider and digest a five-year picture of the government's projected cash flows. Then, after approval by Parliament in aggregate, the projected cash flows should be examined in detail—by the existing sub-committees of the Expenditure Committee which are concerned with such aspects of government activity as Defence, External Affairs, Trade and Industry, and so on; and by the new select committee on financial administration as regards the details of taxation, government borrowing and monetary administration.

In these ways Members of Parliament can satisfy themselves and the public that the government is managing its cash flows so as to meet its multiple responsibilities to society and reconcile the conflicting interests of society's various sections. Decisions about particular patterns and levels of public expenditure, taxation and government borrowing can thus be used to correct the distribution of purchasing power and the allocation of resources that would otherwise take place.

Social and Economic Planning

Most socialist politicians, Keynesian economists, and left-of-centre academics and civil servants have tended to assume that monetary and financial institutions are by nature inefficient and perverse as mechanisms of resource allocation, and therefore as instruments of social and economic planning. They have therefore tried to develop an array of more bureaucratic methods of intervening directly in the market economy. The Conservatives have traditionally been less certain about this, but under Mr Heath's leadership in the early 1970's they appear to have adopted the same approach.

We are exploring the contrary hypothesis, which is as follows. The statutory framework for the activities of business and finance is in need of radical reform. The tax system likewise must be radically changed and simplified. The financial and monetary activities of government must be subjected to more open scrutiny and investigation by Parliament and the public. Senior officials of the Treasury, Governors of the Bank of England, and leading bankers and financiers in the commercial sector should be required to discharge their stewardship for the country's monetary and financial system with a new perception of their public responsibilities. In those conditions, the government's control of its own cash flows under parliamentary supervision could become one of the most powerful instruments of economic and social planning that it would be possible to imagine or devise.

How, then, can we arrange to use cash flow planning and management routines, carried out by government under parliamentary supervision, as instruments of social and economic planning? How are we to develop these routines as mechanisms of collective choice, for allocating resources and distributing purchasing power in a pattern acceptable to all? How shall we use these mechanisms successfully for reconciling conflicting interests and distributing fair shares, instead of attempting to use them unsuccessfully in pursuit of the single objective of maximum economic growth? What arrangements for 'corporate planning' are needed in central government, comparable to those that will be needed in socially responsible enterprises?

As a basis for discussion, let us postulate regular annual arrangements on the following lines. Every year there will be open, public discussions—perhaps in the National Economic Development Council (NEDC)—between representatives of government, industry, trade unions and the financial institutions, about the shifts in economic and social priority that may be desirable over the next few years. These discussions should take account of published economic assessments made by the Treasury for a period of five years ahead. The discussions should also deal with possible future movements in prices and incomes, and in particular with changes in relative incomes that may be desirable for one reason or another over the next few years. Material for discussion should include appraisals of possible future movements in prices and incomes published by a revived Prices and Incomes Board (or the new standing Royal Commission on Prices and Incomes).

These discussions in the NEDC should precede and form part of the background to Parliament's decisions—mentioned earlier—on public expenditure, taxation and borrowing, projected five years ahead and budgeted for the coming year. Those are the decisions that embody the relevant priorities. For example, a decision to channel more resources into education or public transport makes it possible to raise the pay of teachers or railwaymen; while a decision to channel more resources into housing makes it possible to give a bigger subsidy to certain categories of house purchasers, e.g. first time home buyers.

These decisions by Parliament and government will then be translated—through the mechanisms of public spending, taxation and borrowing—into transfers of funds, and therefore transfers of entitlement to purchasing power and the use of society's resources. If the monetary and financial system is operating straight and fair, social and economic priorities thus openly agreed by Parliament will shape the environment for socially responsible enterprises of all kinds, which may then be left to reach their own decisions and shape their own priorities in accordance with it. By this approach to economic and social planning, the government can provide a framework acceptable to society as a whole, in which free enterprise can flourish in the public interest. Thus socially responsible enterprise and financially responsible government will mesh together as the institutions for a socially united and economically prosperous society.

Taxation and Financial Assistance

Taxes are money which society receives from its members; benefits and other forms of financial assistance are money which people receive from society. The system of taxes and social security benefits (and grants and allowances to industry) is the whole set of rules that determines the amounts to be paid. It thus affects the whole pattern of cash flows through society, and forms a vital part of the framework of public policy and regulation in which individual people and corporate enterprises shape their own activities. The system of taxes and benefits ought therefore to be designed as a means of ensuring that the total pattern of cash flows through society reflects and contributes to the achievement of accepted social and economic aims.

Looked at in that light, the present system of taxation and financial assistance is badly designed from almost any point of view. Tax concessions, exemptions, and allowances are unjust, since they give most assistance to those who are already best off and least to those who are worst off. The fact that income is taxed more heavily than increases in wealth encourages people to seek speculative capital gains rather than higher income. It therefore encourages investment in assets like land and property, jewellery and old masters, at the expense of investment in productive enterprise to create new income and wealth for the community. By thus encouraging a flight from money, it helps to stimulate inflation. It favours those who inherit or otherwise take over existing assets against those who create new wealth for themselves and their fellow citizens. High marginal rates of income tax at the top end of the scale are matched by high marginal rates at the bottom end, so that poorer people—like pensioners—are discouraged from working and find themselves locked into a poverty trap.

The fact that companies are taxed on profits paradoxically means that their expenditure benefits from tax relief—unlike expenditure by individual people out of their taxed income, or by the public services out of taxes. This encourages wasteful spending by companies; it unjustly favours organization men in the so-called 'private sector' and arbitrarily distorts the pattern of the economy in favour of 'private' corporate activity against public service and individual enterprise. Moreover, the whole system of taxes and benefits—including tax concessions, exemptions and allowances—has become enormously complex. Its administration constitutes a serious drain on society's resources of talent, many highly qualified specialists being employed either to collect taxes or help taxpayers to avoid them. Furthermore, since only rich individuals and large companies can afford to employ the services of these specialists, the balance is tilted further in favour of the rich against the poor and in favour of the large company against the small. Meanwhile, financial assistance is given to industry by the government in a wide variety of forms, substantially offsetting the revenue taken from companies in taxation. Finally, assistance is given to individuals by the state in a wide variety of different benefits and grants; many of these are subject to means tests; many are administered by different government agencies; in aggregate they appear to fail in their purpose of alleviating poverty and eliminating social injustice and social unrest.

Clearly, it would not have been easy to design a set of rules determining the pattern of payments between society and its members that was better calculated to achieve the wrong results. But, of course, the system has not been designed. It has grown up piecemeal over many years, and it is now ripe for fundamental overhaul.

The time has come to consider the possible advantages of a drastically simplified system. It might consist of three elements:

(1) a progressive annual tax on personal *wealth*,

(2) a substantial turnover tax or consumption tax possibly on the lines of Value Added Tax (VAT), and additional duties on particular goods and services of a special kind, like alcohol, tobacco and gambling—this being, in effect, taxation of *spending*,

(3) substantial flat-rate benefits, universally payable as of right to every eligible citizen (regardless of his wealth or income), in the form of children's and dependants' benefits, students' grants, unemployment benefits, sickness and disability benefits, householders' benefits, pensions, and other similar kinds of benefit—these being, in effect, ways of helping people to meet their *needs*.

The following features of the present system would then disappear.

(a) There would be no corporate taxation,

(b) there would be no taxes on income or capital gains,

(c) there would be no death duties or taxes on gifts and accessions,

(d) there would be no taxes on labour and no social security contributions,

(e) there would be no tax concessions, exemptions or allowances,

(f) there would be no means tests,

(g) there would be no financial assistance to industry.

Such a system could have much to commend it. It would make possible any desired pattern of payments between individuals and the community. By varying the relative rates of payment, it would be possible to change that pattern from time to time in accordance with political philosophies that put different relative emphases on people's wealth, people's spending and people's needs. It would be a much simpler system than we have at present—easier to understand and therefore fairer. It would reflect the extent to which people command and use the resources of society (their wealth and spending), rather than the extent to which they contribute to society's well-being (their income). It would encourage personal enterprise and hard work, and make it possible for young people to acquire personal wealth by saving and investing what they earn. It would reduce inflation by discouraging the flight of money into unproductive assets. It would discourage speculation in land and property—thereby making land more readily available for housing, farming and other economic and social purposes. Such a system of taxation and benefits might even be extended to give cash grants or special credits to individuals for buying education or health services, or to pay members of families to stay at home and look after the young, the sick and the elderly—thereby reversing the present institutionalization of the public services.

Obviously we cannot move overnight to a new tax and social security system on those lines. First, it will have to become accepted that such a reshaping of the system is needed as part of the wider task of reforming the money system to perform its new social role. Next, it will be necessary to examine the proposed system in detail: for example, to explore with the aid of computer models the impact of many different rates of taxes and benefits on the pattern of cash flows through society; and to examine the most practical ways of dealing with the undoubted problems of valuation and assessment. Only then will the third stage be possible—a steady move, through a series of planned steps over a period of years, to the new system.

To bring inflation under control; to stimulate personal enterprise and hard work; to encourage saving and investment in the creation of new wealth and welfare; to promote social justice; and to relieve poverty and distress—those are all aims that Parliament should be striving to achieve, quite apart from the overriding aim of designing the money system as a mechanism of collective choice. It should therefore be a prime responsibility of Parliament in the coming years to speed the examination and introduction of a new system of taxation and financial assistance on some such lines as those suggested here. Unremitting parliamentary and public pressure on the Treasury and the Revenue Departments may be needed, if progress is to be made.

Financial and Monetary Administration

The second of the government's main financial responsibilities—after the planning and management of its own cash flows—is to maintain the efficient and proper working of the monetary and financial system in society at large. Government should be responsible for seeing that the functions of the central monetary authority are carried out and that the financial markets are regulated in the public interest.

The head of the central monetary authority

ought to accept professional responsibility for seeing that the country's monetary and financial system works efficiently and fairly. His first responsibility should be to see that the value of money is maintained, and that monetary inflation is brought under control. He should be asked to make sure, if he can, that monetary inflation is not caused by the 'creation' of too much new money at home, or imported as a result of the declining value of this country's currency in relation to what we have to buy from abroad. He should get his staff to work out whatever new measures may be necessary to enable him to discharge these responsibilities properly.

It may prove desirable to change the present methods of creating new money and regulating interest rates. Perhaps new money should be created only in the form of 'special drawing rights' issued by the central monetary authority itself, and we should stop the credit-creating activities of banks and other financial institutions. On the foreign exchange side, perhaps the central monetary authority should be expected to exercise more stringent controls over the rates prevailing in the foreign exchange market, and over the volumes of business transacted in it. There is surely no point in having a separate currency at all, unless it confers a degree of monetary independence.*

---

* The ideas and suggestions made in this chapter are clearly relevant to the problems of international monetary reform. I suspect that the best hope of real progress in that sphere is to work from the bottom up, by creating honest and efficient domestic monetary systems under the single jurisdiction of individual governments and by evolving those into a similar international system. But this needs further examination.

However, these are technical details. It is for the professional experts to examine them constructively and openly on our behalf. We have a right to know whether the country's money system can provide society and its members with a reliable way of handling their transactions with one another, and with a mechanism for allocating resources and purchasing power according to people's entitlement and their choice. The head of the country's central monetary authority should therefore give a regular account of his stewardship to Parliament and the public, through the proposed new parliamentary select committee on financial administration. If government policies make it impossible for him to carry out his responsibilities, then he should resign. If other factors make it impossible, he should explain publicly what they are and he should put forward proposals for dealing with the situation.

It is not unreasonable to look critically on various aspects of the way in which the British money systems works today. Inflation has been allowed to become self-perpetuating. To some extent this is due to the tax system. But in other ways too the money system has acquired a built-in bias in favour of borrowers against savers. It is also biassed in favour of big people against small, and in favour of those who run the system against those who use it. For example, the government takes deliberate steps to keep down the rate of interest paid to small savers and depositors in National Savings, building societies and banks, to enable itself to raise money below the market rates. And the Bank of England, which is supposed to be responsible as central monetary authority for safeguarding the fair and efficient working of the country's monetary system, is also expected to manage the debts and new borrowing of the government itself on a specially favoured basis!

Patchy regulation of the financial markets leaves the door open to abuse. Self-regulation by the Stock Exchange, for example, prevents free competition and is widely supposed to result in too much of the money handled there being creamed off as fees and commissions. Conflicts of interest exist quite widely, and those who run the financial markets are generally thought to manipulate them in their own favour. Nobody really knows how much cheating takes place. Scandals come to light from time to time, and nasty things crawl out from under stones. But little has to be disclosed, the rules and regulations are obscure, responsibility for administering them is diffuse, and many a stone is left unturned.

In all these various spheres of monetary and financial administration Parliament at present makes little serious attempt to exercise its supervisory and investigatory functions. The Treasury, the Bank of England, and the City of London (and to a lesser extent the Revenue Departments), are allowed to constitute a solid core of closed government at the financial heart of a supposedly democratic society. The government is financially irresponsible, in the strict sense of that word. This state of affairs is wrong. It ought to be put right.

The Law

I noted in the previous chapter that recent developments in consumer protection law, employee protection law, and investor protection (i.e. company) law, together with laws and regulations governing the impact of industry on the environment and other measures protecting the public interest, are gradually building up into a comprehensive statutory framework for business and financial activities.

The coherent development and effective administration of this whole corpus of law is an important task for government. The law is, at present, especially under-developed on the financial side. Investors, depositors, savers, insurance policy holders, borrowers and others who deal with financial institutions, all need increased protection. Industrial relations law has, of course, been a matter of political controversy for some years.

It is, in fact, a revealing symptom of the double standard adopted by top people in Britain at the present time that the Labour and Conservative governments of 1966 and 1970 should both have spent so much energy and lost so much political goodwill in trying to bring the trade unions within the framework of the law. Not even the Labour government seemed to realize the extent to which the industrial and financial establishments were also free from up-to-date statutory controls and open accountability in respect of their public responsibilities. Company law is badly out of date. The City of London proudly maintains the merits of self-regulation—just as the trade unions do—

and has always argued fiercely against statutory controls over banking and the Stock Exchange. It has needed the resistance of the trade unions to the Conservative government's Industrial Relations Act to demonstrate that what is sauce for the trade union goose will have to be sauce for the gander in the boardroom and the banking parlour too. All these big baronies should be brought within an up-to-date framework of law.

That, then, is the way forward on the legal side—to develop the existing fragments of company law, employment law, consumer protection law, and financial and banking law, into a well-designed and coherent framework of regulation for business activity. This will provide the statutory backing for the kind of socially responsible, self-governing enterprise outlined in the previous chapter. Again, it will be Parliament's task to prod the government into accepting its responsibilities. It will also be Parliament's task to satisfy itself that the laws are being properly administered by the government agencies designated for that purpose.

While ministers and officials in the departments of central government (such as Trade, Industry and Employment) should be held responsible for framing the legislation and carrying it through Parliament, the actual administration of the laws and regulations thus created should be devolved to semi-autonomous government agencies. These agencies will include: first, a Companies Commission and a Commission to regulate the activities of banks, the Stock Exchange, insurance, and other financial activities; second, a Commission on Industrial

Relations; and, third, the Directorate-General of Fair Trading. They will thus cover the interests of investors, employees, and customers, and see that all those interests are effectively protected according to the provisions of the law. The situation in which a Labour government insists on a Companies Commission and refuses to have a Commission on Industrial Relations, while a Conservative government insists and refuses vice versa, is just plain absurd.

In the previous chapter I described money as the scoring system and laws as the rules of the game. I suggested that the legitimacy of managements in socially responsible, self-governing enterprises needs to be validated within a framework of control that ensures fair and acceptable treatment for all the parties involved. This chapter has been concerned with the government's responsibilities.

To summarize so far. The government should accept full responsibility for drawing up the rules of the game and administering them; for designing the scoring system and supervising the score-keepers so that the system operates fairly and straight; and for settling social and economic priorities at the national level and seeing to their implementation—using its control of government cash flows as the mechanism of collective decision and action in this respect. The legitimacy of government in discharging these responsibilities must be continually re-established, by discharging them openly under the supervision of Parliament and the public and by securing the consent of Parliament and the public to what is done. If those responsibilities are properly carried out, socially responsible business concerns and financial institutions will be able to act freely within the framework of law and public policy thus laid down, the public interest will be served, and detailed intervention by the government will have become unnecessary. But an honest money system is a prime requirement.

HONEST MONEY

THE new social role of money is to provide society with one of its most important mechanisms of collective choice. In the two previous chapters I have outlined how the planning and control and distribution of flows of money can be used as such a mechanism, first at the level of the enterprise and then at the level of national government. In this chapter I shall try to suggest how the country's money system could be made to work straight and fair.

I have said that the money system is a scoring system. It is a calculus of value, an accounting system, which indicates the entitlements of people (including organizations) to purchasing power and thus enables us to recognize the claims they may make on society's resources. Using the institutions that operate the monetary and financial system (banks, insurance companies, stockbrokers, and so on), people can trade present for future purchasing power over time as suits them best, and prepare themselves or their successors for untoward events such as accident or death. In other words, the monetary and financial system makes it possible for individuals and organizations and society as a whole to channel the resources at their command into the activities of their choice at the time desired.

If we visualize the flows of money that arise from buying, selling, investing, borrowing, insuring, paying taxes, receiving taxes, and so on, we see that these money flows—or cash flows—to and from each individual, to and from each enterprise, and to and from the government itself, reflect the patterns of their activities in relation to one another and the rest of society. By planning and managing those cash flows successfully, all concerned should be able to plan and manage the complex totality of their activities so that they interact acceptably with one another. The government, by planning and managing *its* cash flows successfully should be able to carry out its complex range of tasks coherently, in accordance with social and economic priorities democratically laid down. An enterprise, by planning and managing *its* cash flows successfully should be able to discharge its multiple responsibilities, in accordance with its agreed priorities. An individual, by planning and managing *his* (or her) cash flows successfully, will be helped to pursue his aims and objectives while meeting his various obligations to other members of society.

The money system is, in fact, what economists call a resource allocation system. Every society must have such a system. In totalitarian countries it tends to be highly centralized, operating largely by instructions coming down from the top. In market economies it is decentralized, operating at least in theory through a multitude of independent decisions. In the self-governing democracy of the post-capitalist and post-socialist society, where we want to encourage social responsibility *and* personal enterprise, we shall clearly want the money system to operate fairly, openly and accountably, like the machinery of government itself. We shall want it to reflect the values and honour the due claims of those who use it, whether at the level of society as a whole, at the level of the enterprise, or at the level of the individual. We shall want it to work uncorrupted by the interests and aims of those responsible for running it; and we shall want the latter to be publicly accountable for the way it works.

Lenin had clear ideas about the banking and financial system: 'A single state bank on the largest scale, with branches in every rural district, in every factory—that is already nine-tenths of a socialist apparatus. It means book-keeping for the whole state, measuring and checking the output and distribution of goods for the whole state; it is, so to speak, the framework of a socialist society.' Up to a point that approach is relevant. But as it stands it is altogether unacceptable. Even if it were theoretically desirable, in practice a single centralized state bank is not a feasible proposition. Financial institutions, like other enterprises of all kinds, have to be run by human beings. They will work best and will most effectively provide the financial services needed by their customers and by society, if they operate in an open, plural environment which will enable them to compete fairly with one another and give maximum scope to the energies and aspirations of their employees. Centralized state socialism is no better in practice than socially irresponsible capitalism.

In considering the money system as a scoring system, we have to remember that the game of life differs from games like cricket or football. There the object of the exercise is to make as big a score as possible; comparatively few people dedicate their lives whole-heartedly to making as much money as they can. Most people are content if they maintain their score at an acceptable level. Most people, then, think of money as something that contributes to their needs. They want enough of it to satisfy these needs, and they want to manage its incoming and outgoing conveniently, but they do not want to spend most of their time and energy thinking about it or working at it. For them there are more important things in the game of life than the score, and their most vital relationships with other people are conducted largely outside the cash nexus.

Something similar can be said of most companies and institutions, whatever the traditional theory of the firm asserts. They are in business to make cars or television sets, or to provide an education service or a medical service, or to make some other contribution to the total provision of goods and services that society needs. They are not in business for the primary purpose of making as much money as possible.

It is because most people do not want to spend too much time worrying about the score, that the integrity and reliability of the money system as a scoring system is so important. In examining the financial system from this point of view, five separate functions must be distinguished. I shall discuss these in terms of British financial institutions, but the five-fold division of functions is universally applicable.

First, there is the score-keeping function performed by the current account activities of the clearing banks and the Giro. Second, there is the function of scorekeeper-in-chief performed by the Bank of England as central monetary authority. The clearing banks and the Giro hold accounts for all their customers, and the central monetary authority holds accounts for the clearing banks and the Giro. Between them they thus provide a system for keeping and exchanging scores between all account-holders in the country. It is their job, and especially that of the central monetary authority (which also issues the metal and paper tokens that we call coins and banknotes), to see that the whole scoring system works.

The third function is performed by a wide variety of traders and brokers who create a market in money and financial claims of all kinds. The individuals and companies trading in this market (who include every kind of financial institution ranging from banks, building societies, insurance companies, and unit trusts to stockbrokers) provide a theoretically infinite variety of ways in which a certain amount of money can be paid today for the right to receive a different amount at a later date; or in which, conversely, money can be received today in return for an obligation to repay a different amount later. The actual amount of money to be received (or repaid) later, and the actual date, may be either specified in advance or determined by the occurrence of subsequent events, as agreed in the terms of the bargain. For example, the repayments of a personal loan from a bank or the repayment on maturity of a (without profits) endowment policy will be predetermined both as to amount and as to date. The repayments in respect of a purchase of equity shares or of a building society mortgage will be predetermined as to date, but will be later determined as to amount according to how well the company has done or what the future levels of interest are. The repayment of a life insurance policy is predetermined as to amount, if it is without profits, but its date is determined by the date on which the policy-holder dies. Finally, there are repayments such as those in respect of most insurance policies, in which both the amount and the date of the repayment are determined by the extent of the damage or loss that is suffered and the date on which it occurs.

The logical principles underlying this market in money and financial claims are clearly very simple: money today can be received or paid in exchange for rights to money in the future—the amount, date and conditions of repayment being decided by the terms of each particular bargain. Computer people go so far as to say that, in theory, it might one day be possible to handle every financial transaction through a single computerized system: each bargain could be uniquely described by stating its defining characteristics—the parties to it, the amounts, the timings and the conditions of payment and repayment. At the same time, the system could be straightforwardly controlled; permissible types of transaction could be clearly described in statutes and regulations by reference to their defining characteristics; the constraints thus imposed could be applied in the form of a computerized check on all transactions; and impermissible transactions would be automatically rejected.

For practical purposes in the foreseeable future, ideas of that kind are somewhat far-fetched. Financial institutions evolved historically in a piecemeal, muddled, higgledy-piggledy way, just as one would expect. As a result the money system now consists of a large number of self-created specialisms, complex and difficult for the outsider—the ordinary citizen or businessman or even systems analyst—to understand. Deposit banks, building societies, savings banks, finance houses, insurance companies, pension funds, investment trusts, unit trusts, national savings, merchant banks, issuing houses, discount houses, money market dealers and brokers, stockbrokers and stockjobbers, bondbrokers and bond dealers—these are among the kinds of people and institutions in the City of London that trade in financial claims. Their critics would say that they have woven a web of mystique around their basically simple services; that they have mostly built a good living on the charges—overt or covert—that their customers have been prepared to pay; and that their activities have been shielded for too long by the high priesthood in the Bank of England, protecting them from the prying eyes of the great unwashed. But few people would seriously suggest that we could computerize the lot.

The complexity of the financial markets gives rise to the fourth and fifth functions performed by the financial sector—the provision of financial *advisory* services and financial *management* services to guide organizations and individuals through the money jungle. For many years these services have specialized, for example on investment advice or investment management. Recently the trend has been towards more comprehensive financial advisory and management services. Customers are helped to plan and manage their inflows and outflows of money *as a whole*, taking account of all their potential sources of revenue and all their potential commitments at various future dates.

This reversal of the trend towards specialization marks a turning point in the development of the financial system. In the field of professional financial advice, bankers, accountants, tax lawyers, investment advisers, insurance brokers and financial planning consultants have been trespassing more and more into one another's fields. At the same time the old demarcation lines between different financial institutions (deposit banks, building societies, savings banks, finance houses, merchant banks, insurance companies, unit trusts, pension funds, and so forth) have been breaking down. The 1973 Report on London's Future as an International Financial Centre by the Inter-Bank Research Organization discussed these developments and pointed out one of the main problems they pose: 'The Government will soon be driven to consider how far the present trend towards all-purpose financial institutions should be encouraged and allowed to go. It clearly should not be arrested on the basis of obsolete distinctions between traditionally-labelled financial institutions, whether imposed by restrictive practices on the part of the institutions themselves or by restrictive regulations on the part of Government. New criteria will be needed to determine what kinds of financial business may and may not be carried out by which institutions, based on a fresh review of public policy in regard to such questions as conflict of interest and concentration of economic power.'

I believe that this question of conflicts of interest is of greater importance than the authorities admit. We have distinguished five separate functions in the operation of the country's monetary and financial system: current account banking (or score-keeping); central monetary authority (or score-keeper-in-chief); trading in financial claims; providing financial advice; and providing financial management. If any organization carries out more than one of these five functions there is risk of a conflict of interest leading to unfair practice. This does not necessarily mean that all such combinations of activity should be forbidden. In some cases they certainly should be. In others, full disclosure of the transactions being carried out will probably provide sufficient safeguard against malpractice. But disclosure must be properly enforced.

In exploring these questions in the next few years, reformers of the financial system are likely to find the model of a scoring system a fruitful source of ideas. Game theorists, operational research scientists, and mathematicians with computable models, should be able to investigate how we would set about making the money system work fairly and efficiently if it were a scoring system for a game. There are a number of particular areas on which they might throw light: first, what would be the effects of using different methods to increase the total score available to the competing players (creating credit, increasing the money supply)? Second, which conflicts of interest are harmless and which are not? Third, what prohibitions and conditions should be introduced to regulate such conflicts? And, fourth, what rules—to be adopted in the course of international monetary reform—should govern interchange between one currency (one scoring system) and another? However, the main point is this: if the scoring system is badly designed, if the score-keeping is unfair or inefficient, if the score-keepers and powerful players are suspected of cheating—then the character of a game suffers. In exactly the same way, the quality of the national life deteriorates when people lose confidence in the money system and come to believe that those responsible for operating it are manipulating it in their own interest or are cheating in some other way.

Inflation is a striking example of this. At the time of writing the annual rate of inflation in Britain is between 15 and 20 per cent. It has become self-reinforcing. It is economically damaging and socially unjust. If allowed to gain momentum, it could lead to serious breakdown in the fabric of organized society. What can we do to halt the slide, so that money will retain its value and therefore be able to function as a reliable scoring system and an honest mechanism of collective choice?

Inflation is one of those abstract terms like economic growth or productivity, which tend to conceal more than they explain. It is cause and effect, symptom and disease. One has the impression of problems so widely ramified that no one need accept responsibility for solving them. For this reason we have to clarify what we are aiming at when we talk about inflation. We must try to reduce the problem to manageable form.

Inflation means that the value of money is declining in relation to the goods and services it buys. This is happening because the availability of money is rising faster than the availability of goods and services. That is happening because, in aggregate, society's members are insisting on getting increases in money greater than the increases in goods and services they are creating.

One of the most distinguished of British economists, Lord Robbins, recently remarked that the remedy for inflation is 'to stop the excess of aggregate expenditure which is its cause'. Clearly that statement points us in the right direction, but by itself it does not take us very far. We want to know what to do, in order to stop the excess of aggregate expenditure.

There is surely no hope that esoteric technical measures will provide the answer. The most obvious of these is the suggested return to a gold standard.

More complicated variants of the same idea are that money values should be founded on a mixed package of basic commodities, including such things as gold, oil and wheat. The trouble with these ideas is threefold: they cannot be adopted without the political will to tackle the problems of inflation internationally; they raise tiresome political problems of their own, such as the fact that South Africa and the Soviet Union are the world's two leading producers of gold; and they do not carry conviction with growing numbers of educated and sceptical people, who regard gold as a superstition and dislike the idea of strengthening the powers of the international monetary priesthood.

Then there is 'monetary correction', including 'indexation'. These terms mean that inflation is accepted as a permanent feature of life, but that the monetary values of items like savings, bank deposits, wages, pensions, taxes, rents and so on, right across the board, are adjusted or revalued from time to time to compensate for the fall in the value of money. Brazil is the country usually quoted as having introduced indexation successfully. The claim is made that in Brazil indexation has not only mitigated the effects of inflation so far as particular categories of vulnerable people (like pensioners) are concerned, but has also reduced the rate of inflation generally. On the other hand, 'threshold agreements'—under which wages rise automatically when the cost of living index rises—have recently added to the inflationary spiral in Britain.

One cannot deny that schemes to palliate the symptoms of monetary inflation may be desirable in the short run—including such things as threshold agreements, index-linked savings and pensions, and inflation accounting. But they do raise serious problems of their own, and they can contribute to further inflation. They certainly complicate everything. However, the reason why they cannot work as a general remedy for inflation is simply that they could only work if the underlying problem had been solved already, in which case they would be unnecessary. The reason why the money system (i.e. the scoring system) loses credibility by inflation is that in aggregate we all insist on having more than our fair share; the powers-that-be cannot hold out; and the score-keepers feel they have to print more money. To suppose that the score-keeping authorities would be able to arrange for everybody's score to be adjusted subsequently in the complicated manner proposed under 'indexation', and that this would restore fair play, assumes that the authorities have enough power to insist on fair play in the first place.

A different remedy for inflation is proposed by traditional advocates of monetary control. Rightwing economists and politicians, like Mr Enoch Powell, together with bankers and financiers, tend to argue on the following lines: if the flow of cash through the economy is slowed down by the central monetary authority cutting back on the 'supply' of money, companies will not receive cash flows sufficiently high to enable them to pay all their existing employees. Unemployment will result. Higher levels of unemployment will check inflation, because as customers the unemployed will exert less pressure on prices and as potential workers they will reduce the pressure on salaries and wages. Deflation can thus be imposed.

In the past, it seemed that high levels of unemployment did indeed go together with monetary stability, and low levels of unemployment with high rates of inflation. However, that correlation no longer appears to obtain. More importantly, I do not see how we can justify deliberately creating the social distress and unrest that goes with high unemployment, even for the sake of restoring a stable currency. Conservative economists are right when they say that inflation is an injustice between man and man, and a dishonesty between government and people. But they cannot be right when they propose to cure it by inflicting a further injustice on millions of vulnerable people. The remedy must involve the creation of a fair and honest money system. That implies an end to profit maximization as a principle of business activity, together with the changes in the tax system and other reforms of financial administration proposed in the previous chapter. Responsible action by the central monetary authority will then take its place as one of a number of measures contributing to socially responsible enterprise, financially responsible government, and an honest money system. To clinch the matter, the Powellite remedy is now impracticable. For the present, the trade unions hold the dominant political power in our society. They simply will not accept the 'I'm all right, Jack', 'devil take the hindmost' philosophy of the banking and financial establishment and the right-wing politicians.

The three proposed remedies for the problem of inflation that I have briefly discussed—gold, indexation, and monetary deflation—have one thing in common which stultifies them all. They are imposed solutions. They assume the existence of powers-that-be possessing the authority to solve the problem *from outside*. But our society is no longer like that. Solutions must come from within. Unless they come in the form of self-controls, they will not come at all.

These self-controls are those I have outlined already—at the level of the enterprise, in government, and in the money system itself. The only cure for inflation is to establish methods of business management, methods of settling social and economic priorities including relative incomes, and methods of dealing with money and financial claims, that are widely accepted as reliable and fair. This involves reforming all our main economic institutions—business, finance, government, and commercial law—so that they constitute a valid institutional framework for self-governing people. This will enable people to satisfy themselves that what is being done is fair. Only then will they be prepared to desist from the inflationary struggle to keep up with the Jones's, in order to make sure of getting fair shares—or more than fair shares—for themselves. An honest money system will only be restored in a society which is seen to be just and fair.

MONEY SCIENCE AND MONEY METAPHYSICS

KEYNES' judgement, that 'practical men who believe themselves to be quite exempt from any intellectual influence, are usually the slaves of some defunct economist', will no doubt continue to be true at least for some time. Nonetheless, I have suggested that a scientific revolution in government and finance is taking place. Moreover, I believe that the new conceptual model of the money system which I am putting forward is genuinely scientific. Inevitably, therefore, in developing this model we must expect to have to jettison a good deal of intellectual lumber in the shape of metaphysical notions inherited from the pre-scientific past. Among these notions are 'profit' and 'economic growth'; 'capitalism' and 'socialism'; the 'mixed economy' or 'split society', with the 'public' and 'private' sectors defined in their present form; and the strange idea that extractive and manufacturing industries make wealth, while service industries and occupations consume it. Even the idea, implied by the use of terms like 'money flows' and 'cash flows', that money is a physical stuff with physical characteristics like 'velocity' and 'supply' will become suspect, once we accept that the money system is an accounting and decision system.

Schumacher has said, 'The task of our generation, I have no doubt, is one of metaphysical reconstruction.' That applies to money no less than to other aspects of the man-made world. Let me try to suggest the kind of thing it will mean.

Lord Kelvin's famous saying, 'When you can measure what you are speaking of and express it in numbers, you know that on which you are discoursing, but when you cannot measure it and express it in numbers, your knowledge is of a very meagre and unsatisfactory kind,' applies to the sphere of action, no less than the sphere of knowledge—to the affairs of society, no less than those of natural science. If we are to make collective choices in complex social and economic affairs, we need a common quantitative calculus of value. The money system is that calculus. If our choices are to be valid, the calculus must be reliable. It must work straight.

At first sight, the fact that money values are man-created may seem to make it difficult to take a scientific view of money at all. But in the physical sciences, too, there are problems about establishing standard measures of distance, time and weight on which the validity of physical measurements can be based. It is true that establishing the validity of the money system has always proved much more difficult, but that is no reason for not approaching the problem scientifically. In the past the validity of money values has often rested on superstition and authority. In our more sceptical and democratic age the validity of the money system can be established only by widespread public agreement that it does indeed work fairly and reliably as a mechanism of collective choice. That is now the way, and the only way, that money values can be established as 'correct'. In a self-governing society the money system must be self-validating, as must the system of government itself. That must be the starting point for a scientific understanding of the money system.

Scientific revolutions threaten the institutional infallibility of the priesthood. It is not wholly frivolous to pursue that thought in the present context.

Where the money system is concerned, at least in Britain, the priesthood consists of three main orders: there are Treasury officials and other officials of central government; there are the central bankers in the Bank of England; and there are the financial wizards in the City of London. The priesthood is supported by various theological schools, of which the Keynesian and monetary economists are probably the most important. Finally, there is a variety of well-paid craftsmen acolytes, including commercial bankers, commercial lawyers and accountants.

According to existing standards of public and professional life, most Treasury officials, Bank of England staff, City people, economists, bankers, lawyers and accountants are people of intelligence and ability whose sense of public and professional responsibility is high. Given the present system, no one would be likely to do better, and there is no need to find fault with them. One understands the practitioners' insistence on working in a closed and secretive environment and one sympathizes with their insecurity at the prospect of change. Treasury officials, for example, genuinely fear that, if they were to publish their forecasts of future rises in incomes and prices, they would thereby accelerate the rising trend. Basically, theirs is an authoritarian philosophy. They are accustomed to do their best in a closed system. Even when it begins to break down, they genuinely fear that an open system would be worse. Similarly, one respects the intellectual subtlety and stamina of the theoreticians. Given that we are not yet institutionally equipped to handle economic problems satisfactorily, economists should not be criticized personally for doing the best they can.

At the same time, the idea that today's financial and economic experts are at the priestly, pre-scientific stage in the development of their calling is attractive.

The defensive attitudes of the Treasury, the Bank of England and the City of London can be interpreted as typical of a self-perpetuating priesthood in decline. They seem to have reacted with undisguised hostility in the 1960's and 1970's to various attempts to penetrate the mumbo jumbo and crack the closed systems of public and commercial finance. They have had to be winkled and bludgeoned along the road towards a more open system. Disclosure of 'true profits' by the big banks and the publication of accounts by the Bank of England had to be politically imposed. In many ways it is remarkable that in a democracy the

Treasury, the Bank of England and the City of London should have been allowed to work in secret for so long.

Turning now to the economists, it is not unfair to the Keynesians to say that they have been sceptical about the importance of money. They have largely ignored the monetary and financial system as a mechanism of social choice and resource allocation, because it has worked so badly. They have concentrated on developing new decision procedures, in parallel with the money system, based on such concepts as 'real' resources, 'real' goods and services, 'real' growth, and 'cost/benefit' analysis. Unfortunately, since money is the only possible 'language' available to human beings for discussing social and economic values quantitatively with precision, the Keynesian economists have been unable to break through the language of money to a world of 'real' values, however hard they have tried. They have been up against an impenetrable conceptual barrier similar to the one encountered by the philosopher Wittgenstein. Understandably they have ignored Wittgenstein's advice, 'whereof thou canst not speak, thereof thou shouldst keep silent'. But, as a result, they have created a fantasy world of economics. They have learned to solve its problems, but not those of the world in which we actually live.

The monetarists seem to have been caught up in somewhat different, though nonetheless misleading, metaphysical assumptions: first, that money is to be studied as a physical commodity; second that the important thing is to measure and analyse how the money system of the day actually works; and third that monetary problems can be solved without changing the decision-making systems actually used in the real-life world of institutions, people and politics. As a result, the abstruse calculations and heated discussions of twentieth-century monetarists about the 'velocity' and 'supply' of money are sometimes reminiscent of the disputes of the medieval schoolmen about the physical attributes of angels.

Thus both main schools of economists, Keynesians and monetarists, appear to have become sidetracked into out-of-date metaphysics, though in rather different ways. Neither kind of economists have become monetary systems engineers. If a cybernetic model of the money system is adopted, according to which money is one of the regulating mechanisms of a self-regulating society, the economic scientists of the future will have to be monetary and financial reformers. Their prime concern will be to improve the money system as an accounting system for society.

We now turn to profit and economic growth. Arguments normally revolve round whether these are good or bad. I believe that such arguments are becoming increasingly meaningless, and that the notions of profit and economic growth are becoming increasingly irrelevant to the modern world. This is because they are metaphysical notions, reflecting the circumstances of the past but not the reality of the present.

When the world still seemed very large and the

activities of men were small in comparison, the idea of profit was developed to account for what happened in agriculture and merchant venturing. During one season the farmer could certainly create a surplus; if the harvest was successful, he had more corn and cattle at the end than at the beginning. During one voyage the merchant venturers could create a surplus too; if they were fortunate, their ship returned full of pepper or silver of a considerably greater value than their outlay. In the early days of the industrial revolution the factory owner was operating not unlike the farmer or the merchant venturer—as an outside intruder in an open-ended world of markets and resources with no apparent limits to growth. He too was hoping to take more out of the system than he put in. So the idea of profit was extended to manufacturing operations too. In due course it was extended by analogy to society as a whole, in which context it became known as 'economic growth', the assumption being that we can *all* get more out of the system than we put in.

The modern world, however, is quite unlike that of 400 years ago. So are the organized activities of people. The fabric of modern society is closely interdependent, and it is now accepted that the world's resources are limited. Human society must therefore operate as a finite system made up of closely interlocking elements, not as if its members were individual particles in open-ended space. In these circumstances the ideas of profit and economic growth cannot be universally applied. Profit and economic growth could only be achieved by some people—and by some generations—at the expense of others. In these circumstances it seems sensible to discard the idea that it is possible to make something out of nothing, to create a surplus of value over and above what existed before. It will be better to adopt the contrary assumption that a business, in transforming labour and materials into a product or a service, cannot create a value greater than the total value of human effort, raw materials, machinery, premises and land that are used or used up in the transformation process. Significantly, the idea that a transformation process can give off a 'surplus', and create values greater than those existing previously, runs directly counter to normal scientific thinking. For example, we all accept that according to the laws of thermodynamics new energy values cannot be created; what happens is that existing energy is transformed or transferred.

In practice, of course, accountants and economists are already finding profit and economic growth more and more difficult to quantify satisfactorily. The difficulties that arise in calculating them, in reaching a 'true and fair view' of profits and in establishing the 'costs of economic growth', are well documented. In particular, the methods used for calculating national income and national product are full of absurdities. Moreover, as calculated, profits and economic growth both appear to have been declining, or failing to rise fast enough, at least in Britain. Conventionally, this is regarded as a serious failure. But future historians may well interpret it in a different light—as a half-conscious shift towards a new set of institutional goals and concepts.

Against that background the conflict between capitalism and socialism becomes as pointless as the old religious wars. The conflict has been about who shall be entitled to the supposed surplus created by industrial activity: does the surplus derive from the contribution made by capital? or from the contribution made by labour? But if we decide that the concept of a surplus is redundant, that conflict becomes redundant too. The cash flowing into an organization must be kept in balance with the cash flowing out, and procedures are required for distributing the outgoing cash flows fairly among all concerned. Accept that convention, and you have the conceptual basis for a post-capitalist and post-socialist society.

The materialist philosophies of capitalism and socialism have both held that to extract the world's resources and manufacture things is to create wealth, whereas to provide services for people is to spend wealth. Today this looks like yet another metaphysical notion which should be firmly discarded. It is related to, though it only partly corresponds to, the supposed distinction between the public and private sectors. The proposal that taxation should be limited to taxes on spending, together with a tax on personal wealth, will help to dissolve both distinctions. I am not arguing dogmatically that the provision of services to people is to be more highly valued than the production of material things, though in advanced countries the future may well lead in that direction. I am simply saying that individuals, organizations, and (at government level) society as a whole, ought to be allowed to allocate their resources and distribute their purchasing power between goods and services as they decide is best. Their choices should not be distorted by institutional factors based on the metaphysics of the past.

A valid money system, as I have said, will evolve only as part of a valid institutional framework for a self-governing society. Our exploration of the new social role of money has thus been largely concerned with the second order questions lying behind politics, government, business and finance. The theme has been that business and finance should be institutions for reconciling multiple interests of a specific kind rather than institutions for pursuing single objectives of a nebulous kind. There is a direct counterpart in the parliamentary and political sphere. To illustrate it I refer to Britain only, but comparable developments have been taking place elsewhere. The underlying stresses and changes are world-wide.

British politics in recent years has been based on a two-party system. The party of capitalism and big business has opposed the party of socialism and the big trade unions. During such a period of time the two-party system comes to be accepted as part of the natural order. The adversary system is supposed to give 'strong' government.

At the time of writing, the whole political spectrum in Britain is confused. The Conservative party is disorientated. The Asquithian parliamentary Liberals are at odds with the community activists at the grassroots level in their party. The Labour party's façade of unity and moderation has cracked and deep divisions are apparent between the reforming social democrats on the one hand and the so-called Marxists and hardline trade unionists on the other. The nationalist movements in Scotland, Wales and Northern Ireland are now more strongly represented in the Westminster parliament than ever before, and no one quite knows what they are going to do.

It seems quite likely that we are entering a period of multi-party parliamentary government. Parliament's role will then be to reconcile a multiplicity of specific interests, maintain a continuing balance between them, and thereby validate the administration of the day—much as supervisory boards in business will be expected to validate the role of management. The death throes of the old metaphysics will thus be seen in the Houses of Parliament and on the hustings, as well as in the boardrooms of industry, the banking parlours of the City, and the corridors of Whitehall.

We conclude this discussion with a reference to political philosophy. Among political philosophers it seems that the ideas of justice and fairness are now taking precedence as the basic political ideas, over the idea of utilitarianism in its various forms. According to utilitarianism, a society is thought to be 'rightly ordered, and therefore just, when its major institutions are arranged so as to achieve the greatest net balance of satisfaction summed over all the individuals belonging to it'. Utilitarianism thus proposes a single objective—to maximize the *net balance of satisfaction*, which is a nebulous metaphysical concept rather like profits or economic growth. With John Rawls I prefer the idea of justice as fairness. I agree with him that 'a just social system defines the scope within which individuals must develop their aims, and it provides a framework of rights and opportunities and the means of satisfaction within and by the use of which these ends may be equitably pursued'. This is a system with multiple objectives. It is not far removed from what Ivan Illich has described as 'an institutional framework which constantly educates to action, participation and self-help'. It accords with the ideas put forward here about business, government and the money system.

P.S. When money is performing its proper role as a fair and efficient mechanism of social choice, what happens to Keynesian 'demand management'? Intuitively, I feel that demand management becomes obsolete. Indeed, I suspect that it is a dangerous distraction from the genuine problems, if not a positively de-stabilizing feature of the present system. Perhaps the supposed need for demand management will simply disappear. Capacity for self-control will have evolved at every decision point in the industrial economy. That should automatically result in decentralized countercyclical decisions. But this is one of the questions that needs further thought and analysis.

WHOSE MOVE?

As Tom Paine said, 'There never yet was any truth or any principle so irresistibly obvious that all men believed it at once.' But when we ask, 'Profit or people?', surely the answer is clear. And not only one kind of people, or people seen in one dimension only, like 'workers' or 'investors'; people of all kinds; and people in all their roles—as workers, customers, investors, residents, holiday-makers, parents, patients, students, teachers, travellers. The new social function of money is to serve whole people; indeed, its function is to help to make them whole, by providing a social value system against which they can integrate their multiple objectives and multiple roles through time. Money's function is also to serve our whole society and help to make it whole. Money is a device for interfacing co-operation with competition. Money is one of the main social mechanisms—others being government and the law—that enable us to reconcile our interests with those of our fellow citizens, resolve the differences between us, and agree upon collective decisions and collective choices.

We have seen that for money to carry out this

function effectively, certain changes are necessary. The divisive notion that businesses exist to maximize profits for shareholders must be replaced by the integrating idea that businesses (and other organizations) provide a framework in which people can create benefits together and share them fairly. The divisive notion that the money system exists to make money for those who run it, must be replaced by the integrating idea that its function is to provide society with a mechanism of collective choice. The divisive notion that it is the government's primary function to maximize economic growth, and that the social services should take second place, must be replaced by the integrating idea that government's function is to enable us to allocate society's resources, and distribute claims upon them, according to values that are generally agreed and accepted.

I have tried to sketch the kind of institutional developments in business, finance and government that will embody these changes of perception. At the political level, it is clear that we are talking of a coherent, evolutionary programme of reform that will lead us towards a post-capitalist and post-socialist society. In essence its aim will be to develop institutional procedures for socially responsible self-government and self-direction at every level of society and in every walk of life.

Pessimists say that fundamental changes of this kind cannot be achieved in an evolutionary way. The people best placed to frame a reform programme of this kind and carry it through have a vested interest in the status quo, or are prisoners of the system which is to be changed. The old system will have to break down in chaos before we can break through to a new one.

Sometimes I am tempted to share that pessimistic view. In a sense it is true that most people in positions of power and influence in Britain today have some kind of vested interest in the existing system of politics, business and government, including the present money system. However honourable they may be personally, most Conservative and Labour politicians are climbing career ladders that seem to rest on the confrontation politics of greed on the right and envy on the left; most bankers and financiers probably do have a vested interest in preserving a closed and unfair financial system; it is natural enough for top civil servants to resist the thought that they have spent their working lives in a closed and muddled system of government which is now ripe for reform; big businessmen do have a vested interest in maintaining closed autocratic methods of company management; and top trade union leaders clearly have a vested interest in industrial conflict, since it is what gives them their opportunity to make their way in life. Meanwhile, it is not easy for the younger people in politics, the City, Whitehall, industry and the trade unions to speak up; efforts to reform the system from within can all too easily result in ejection from it. The policy research institutions, the business schools and the powerful consultancy organizations of the 'think industry' depend on the goodwill of the existing system for their funds, and so they cannot question it too deeply. Finally, the private individuals best endowed with the intelligence and energy to press for changes in the existing system are also those best able to avoid its damaging effects and even to profit from its distortions. Personal commitments and family responsibilities often weigh heavily on them. It is not easy for them to act against the existing system or, if they do so, to be sure that they are doing right.

There is enough force in those arguments to make necessary to ask where the pressures for evolutionary reform will come from. For, as Harold Laski said, vested interests do not abdicate before logic.

Will pressure come from a middle-class backlash against big business, big government and big trade unions? From organized consumers, students, parents, patients and commuters? From women and women's organizations? From geographically-based interests, ranging from Scottish and Welsh nationalists to local amenity groups and residents' associations? From conservationists? From Milovan Djilas' 'new class' of managers and professional people, demanding a re-validation of their roles on a firm basis of social responsibility? It seems probable that as they organize themselves more strongly, interest groups like these will generate some of the necessary pressure for change. Together with the kind of people who think of themselves as liberals and social democrats—and even Powellites—in politics, they are likely to cut increasingly across traditional party alignments. This will help.

But of course there are also many people in the mainstream of business, finance and government, including the two big political parties, who are concerned with the well-being of society as well as with more parochial and sectional interests, such as those of big business or the big trade unions. It would be unfair to think otherwise. More and more of them are likely to turn their attention to the need to develop the institutional mechanisms for a fair, self-governing society. Among these they will probably give a high priority to the money system. Conservative supporters have recently been reminded of Lenin's advice (or was it Keynes'?) that 'if you want to destroy capitalism, first debauch the currency'. Labour supporters are beginning to sense that the only way to articulate 'the language of priorities' is through a socially responsible money system. A pleasing paradox thus presents itself: as the parties of capitalism and socialism turn their attention to reforming the money system as an instrument of their own political philosophy, they will find that they are helping us steadily along the road towards the post-capitalist and post-socialist society of the future.

So what happens next?

No single mind at a single point in time can lay down detailed proposals for developing large ideas and putting them into action. Those who 'see in imagination the things that might be and the way in which they are to be brought into existence' must communicate their insights to one another as best they can. Like Mao Tse-tung, each has his own particular contribution to make to the never-ending process of 'continuous development from the realm of necessity to the realm of freedom'.

To transform the money system into a fair and efficient mechanism of collective choice—a value system for society—will be one such contribution. It must be pioneered by those of us who can imagine what the new social role of money could be and how it may be achieved. We shall be cutting across established institutions and established schools of thought. The initiative rests with us.

BIBLIOGRAPHY

CHARDIN, Pierre Teilhard de, *The Phenomenon of Man*. Collins, 1959.
DERRICK, P. and PHIPPS, J. F., *Co-ownership, Co-operation and Control*. Longmans, 1969.
DJILAS, Milovan, *The Unperfect Society; Beyond the New Class*. Methuen, 1969.
HERZBERG, Frederick, *The Motivation to Work*. John Wiley & Sons, Inc., 1959.
HUMBLE, John, *Social Responsibility Audit*. Foundation for Business Responsibilities, 1973.
ILLICH, Ivan, *Celebration of Awareness*. Calder & Boyars, 1971.
—— *Deschooling Society*. Calder & Boyars, 1971.
Inter-Bank Research Organization, *The Future of London as an International Financial Centre*. HMSO, 1973.
JONES, Aubrey, *The New Inflation: The Politics of Prices and Incomes*. André Deutsch, 1973.
KOESTLER, Arthur, *The Act of Creation*. Hutchinson, 1964.
KUHN, T. S., *The Structure of Scientific Revolutions*. Chicago U.P., 1962.
MCRAE, Hamish and CAIRNCROSS, Frances, *Capital City*. Eyre Methuen, 1973.
MISHAN, E. J., *The Costs of Economic Growth*. Pelican Books, 1969.
NICHOLSON, Max, *The Big Change*. McGraw Hill, 1973.
RAWLS, John, *A Theory of Justice*. Oxford University Press, 1971.
REICH, Charles A., *The Greening of America*. Penguin Books, 1970.
ROBERTSON, James, *Reform of British Central Government*. Chatto & Windus and Charles Knight, 1971.
SCHUMACHER, E. F., *Small is Beautiful*. Blond & Briggs, 1973.
Social Audit, Munro House, 9 Poland Street, London W.1.
THE ECOLOGIST, *A Blueprint for Survival*. Penguin Books, 1972.
The Responsibilities of the British Public Company. Confederation of British Industry, 1973.